ELIE WIESEL

KING SOLOMON AND HIS MAGIC RING

PAINTINGS BY
MARK PODWAL

GREENWILLOW BOOKS
NEW YORK

Gouache, acrylics, and colored pencils were used for the full-color art.
The text type is Kuenstler 480 BT.

Library of Congress Cataloging-in-Publication Data
Wiesel, Elie, (date)
King Solomon and his magic ring / by Elie Wiesel ; illustrated by Mark Podwal.
    p.   cm.
Summary: Recounts some of the stories of the wisdom and folly
in the life of the legendary King Solomon.
ISBN 0-688-16959-7
1. Solomon, King of Israel—Juvenile literature.   2. Bible. O.T.—Biography—
Juvenile literature.   3. Jews—Kings and rulers—Biography—Juvenile literature.
[1. Solomon, King of Israel.   2. Bible stories—O.T.]   I. Podwal, Mark H., (date) ill.
II. Title.   BS580.S6W45   1999   222′.5309′2—dc21   [B]
98-45433   CIP   AC

FOR ELISHA, ALWAYS
—E. W.

FOR SUSAN HIRSCHMAN
—M. P.

KING
SOLOMON
AND
HIS MAGIC
RING

Come, children. Come and listen.

I want to share with you strange yet marvelous tales of a very

great king whom the world admired. Only the demons were

jealous of him. . . .

9

His name was Solomon, or *Shlomo* in Hebrew, which could mean that he was a man of peace *(shalom)*, or a man who sought perfection *(shleimut)*. Or both.

A son of King David, the warrior, he assumed his father's throne when he was just a boy of twelve. But Solomon's own reign was peaceful, and it remained so for forty years.

Some believe God chose Solomon to build the great Temple in Jerusalem because he was a man of peace. Others believe that by choosing Solomon over his father, God was punishing David for shedding so much blood. Still others think the father's loyalty to God was being rewarded: How many fathers had sons who had been asked to build the House of the Lord?

God loved the young king so much that He spoke to him in his dreams. "I will grant you whatever you wish," God told Solomon. When the king responded by asking only for wisdom, the Lord was pleased. "I will also give you what you did not ask," said He. "I will give you riches and glory too."

Not only was Solomon the wisest of all rulers, he was also the mightiest. Some claim he ruled the entire world. Have you heard about the magic ring that the Angel Michael gave to him?

One day the angel brought Solomon a simple ring with a seal made from an engraved stone. "Take this gift which God has sent you," said the angel. "With it you will conquer all the demons of this world, and with their labor, you shall build the Temple in Jerusalem."

From the moment he slipped the ring on his finger, Solomon's authority extended over everything from spirits and animals to the wind. And, as Michael had promised, even the demons became his servants. They carried water all the way from India for the exotic plants that bloomed in Solomon's magnificent gardens. Indeed, Solomon's powers were so great that as long as he lived, the moon remained full.

Solomon's words were undisputed. His judgments became law. All the kings of the earth rushed to Jerusalem to learn from him. Many sent their sons to serve as his scribes.

Solomon's favorite pastime? He loved to play chess— the game that some say he invented. Naturally, his record was unrivaled. He never lost a single match.

14

His means of travel? The king flew upon a huge carpet of green silk that was braided with gold. This carpet, sixty miles long and equally wide, took him swiftly to the farthest corners of the earth. In a single day, Solomon could have dinner at one end of his vast kingdom and dessert at the other.

Solomon loved speaking with animals, and with the help of his magic ring, he became acquainted with the language of all living things from the birds of the sky to the fish in the sea to the wild beasts of the field. Deer escorted his chariot. Lions and tigers carried his armor. Some animals even stood in line outside the royal kitchen to await the honor of being his dinner.

Indeed, Solomon was such a friend to the animals that they would often come to him to settle their disputes. Occasionally, it was the animals who helped Solomon.

Listen:

Once, on a very hot day, Solomon summoned the eagles to shield his soldiers from the rays of the sun. The eagles extended their wings, and instantly, day turned into night. Puzzled, King Hiram quickly ordered his army to retreat. And so, thanks to these creatures, a war ended before it began.

Another story:

In the Valley of the Ants, one ant ordered the others to flee so as not to be trampled by Solomon's soldiers. Upon hearing this command, Solomon told his men to halt and summoned the ant that had spoken.

18

The queen ant crawled out of her palace, and Solomon asked her, "Is there anyone greater in the world than I?" She refused to answer until the king agreed to place her in his hand and raise her up to his face.

Solomon obliged her and repeated his question: "Is there anyone greater in the world than I?"

"Yes!" replied the queen ant.

"Who?" asked the incredulous king.

"I!" said the ant.

Seeing the disbelief in Solomon's face, she explained, "If I were not greater than you, then why did you obey me?"

Solomon did not answer. What could he have said? A truly wise person knows when to listen and when to be silent.

20

This time a story involving birds:

Said one bird to the other, "If you wish, I will destroy the great tower on which the king is now standing." Indignant, Solomon, who had overheard the conversation, ordered the boastful bird to his throne. "How dare you!" he scolded. "You are small and weak. The stones are big and heavy." Unafraid, the bird answered, "Have you forgotten that one says all kinds of foolish things to impress one's beloved?" Solomon was wise enough to smile.

22

Once, while the king was drinking wine and the demons were dancing for his guests, Solomon was approached by his favorite bird, the hoopoe. "For three months I've been searching for a place you do not rule," said the bird. "Finally, I discovered the Kingdom of Sheba. There, water flows from paradise itself, and gold is as abundant as sand. This kingdom is ruled by a beautiful queen, and if you will permit me, I will fly there and bring her to you."

Having heard so much about Solomon's fame, the Queen of Sheba accepted the hoopoe's invitation. The journey from her kingdom to Jerusalem? Usually, it took seven years. But in her eagerness, the queen arrived at Solomon's palace in less than half that time. Her caravan brought hundreds of precious gifts—gold, spices, and jewels—for the king.

24

Solomon received her while sitting on his splendid gold-and-ivory throne. To the left and the right of each of the six steps leading to it, a golden lion and a golden eagle faced one another. The seventy members of the Sanhedrin, or Supreme Council, sat before the throne, which was surrounded by seventy thousand chairs for princes, sages, and judges. Perhaps what was most unusual about the throne was that it followed Solomon wherever he went.

The Queen of Sheba was breathless at what she beheld. But she was most impressed by Solomon's legendary wisdom. He effortlessly solved all of her most difficult riddles. There was nothing he did not know.

The Queen of Sheba had intended to conquer Solomon. Instead, she was conquered by love.

The most glorious event in Solomon's life was surely the building of the Temple. His whole kingdom—indeed, the whole universe—was called upon to help. And as the Angel Michael had promised, even the demons who dug the Temple's foundation became willing laborers through the powers of the magic ring. Three thousand foremen supervised the ceaseless toil of one hundred fifty thousand workers. Astonishingly, in the seven years it took to complete the Temple, there were never any quarrels or protests, sicknesses or broken tools to delay the work.

The wood that was used? Great trees of cedar and cypress were floated down the sea, all the way from Lebanon. And the stones? According to legend, the heaviest stones moved on their own and set themselves into the walls. The cornerstone of the Temple was so

30

heavy it had to be lifted out of the Red Sea by a spirit. His assistants? The demons, of course.

Iron tools were forbidden in the building of the Temple, because iron was used for weapons of war. Thus, to cut the stones, Solomon needed the *shamir*, a magical worm that could bore through metals, rocks, even diamonds. But Solomon learned from the king of demons, Ashmedai, that it had been hidden by a bird. The bird used the *shamir* to cleave rocks in the mountains so she could plant seeds in them. Wise as ever, Solomon ordered the bird's nest covered with glass, so that the bird would be forced to fetch the *shamir* to get into her own nest.

Did Solomon acquire his wisdom from heaven? Yes. But heaven uses messengers. Shimei, son of Gera, was one of them. He was Solomon's devoted teacher. As long as he lived, his pupil never strayed. It was only after Shimei's death that the king forgot some of his teachings and became weakened by the trappings of power. For instance, Solomon had too many horses—more than the number the Bible says a king should own. He amassed too much gold and silver; even everyday utensils were made of precious metals. He had too many wives — some say as many as one thousand.

Solomon's worst mistake? His marriage to the daughter of Pharaoh. The rejoicing over the king's wedding was greater than the celebration marking the completion of the Temple. Indeed, both events occurred on the very same day. In heaven, there was understandable dismay. "Couldn't the wedding have been postponed?" asked the angels. At that moment, God angrily decided that Solomon's Temple would one day have to be destroyed.

Then Pharaoh's daughter did the unthinkable. She brought her idols into Solomon's palace. While a thousand musicians played their instruments, she performed eighty different dances to keep Solomon under her spell. Above their bed, she spread a canopy in which diamonds and other precious stones were set like stars. Solomon, believing it was still night, overslept.

Meanwhile, the people of Jerusalem were plunged into grief, for they could not open the gates to the Temple. Solomon kept the keys under his pillow, and no one dared wake him. Finally, his servants ran to his mother, Bath-Sheva, for help. What she told her son was not pleasant to his ears: "Your father was a man who feared God; now people will say that if you choose to follow the wrong path, it is my fault."

From that night on, Solomon's own star began to fade.

Another tale:

Ashmedai, the king of demons, had been enslaved by Solomon with the power of his magic ring to help with the building of the Temple. So envious of Solomon was Ashmedai that he constantly dreamt of stealing Solomon's kingdom. Eventually, he succeeded.

38

You may wonder: How could Solomon, the wisest man on earth, be so careless as to let a stranger, a wicked stranger, seize his golden throne? Here, Solomon had only his curiosity to blame.

Because the king enjoyed discussing many subjects with the demon, he refused to release him even after the Temple was completed. One day, the enchained Ashmedai said to Solomon, "Noble king, you are obviously capable of explaining everything in the world because of the magic ring you wear. If you let me have it for a moment, I will show you something you never would have thought possible."

Some say no sooner did Solomon hand the demon his ring than Ashmedai swallowed it. Others say he threw it into the sea. Either way, the demon managed to remove his chains. And when he stretched, one wing touched heaven while the other brushed the ground.

Ashmedai's first act? To exile Solomon, hurling him to a land four hundred miles away. Then Ashmedai turned himself into a Solomon look-alike, assuming his identical appearance, the same light in the eyes, the same voice. He could even mimic Solomon's way of questioning and listening, of eating, walking, and sleeping.

Ashmedai sat on Solomon's throne for three years, and the nation did not even know it.

These three years were very humbling for Solomon. "Before, I used to rule over Israel," moaned the exiled king. "Now all I rule over is my cane!" Some say this was punishment for the three sins he had committed: too many wives, too many horses, too much silver and gold.

Solomon wandered throughout the world from town to town, from house to house, begging for food and knocking on people's doors, saying, *"Ani Shlomo*, I am Solomon . . ."* But the people merely laughed, treating him like a madman. Still, he kept repeating, "I am Solomon." "You?" people said. "Don't be foolish. As you speak this nonsense, King Solomon proudly sits upon his throne, wisely conducting the affairs of his kingdom."

Eventually, Solomon reached the capital of the Ammonite nation where, taken prisoner by the king's cook, he was forced to work in the royal kitchen. When the cook was sick, Solomon prepared a meal for the king that was so delicious, he was appointed in the cook's place.

Naturally, the king's daughter fell in love with Solomon. Furious, her father banished both of them from his land. The two walked for months until they arrived at the sea. There, they lived in poverty. One day, Solomon caught a fish and gave it to his wife to cook. Inside this fish she found . . . the lost ring.

Can you imagine their joy? The instant Solomon put the ring back on his finger, both he and his wife were restored to the palace in Jerusalem. And so Solomon recovered his throne and his identity. And Ashmedai? What did he recover? Only his chains.

And yet Solomon was never quite the same. So fearful was he that Ashmedai would trick him again that he needed sixty warriors to guard his bed. Unless they were there, he could not fall asleep.

Little has been recorded about Solomon's last days. Had he become sad? Lonely? Remorseful, perhaps?

Our sages tell us that at the end of his life, his magic ring became more important to him than ever. Whenever he was unhappy, he had only to put it on his finger to find joy again. And if for some reason he felt too happy, he had only to remove it from his finger. Three Hebrew words were engraved on the inside of the ring: "*Gam zu yaavor*—that, too, shall pass."

When Solomon died, his kingdom broke apart.

Imagine: his son Rehavam gave the golden throne— the pride of his late father's palace—to Pharaoh as a gift. That is what some ancient sources say. But then, they say so many things.

What remains of King Solomon's legacy?

His heirs became enemies. His Temple? It lay in ruins.

And the magic ring? Sadly, it has vanished.

But one thing remains.

His wisdom.

In his books.

Come, children. Come and read.

A Note on Sources

Solomon, son of King David and Bath-Sheva, reigned in the tenth century B.C.E. as the third king of Israel. The biblical accounts of the visit by the Queen of Sheba, the building of the Temple, and Solomon's renown as the wisest of men can be found in 1 Kings.

Tradition attributes to Solomon the writing of three books of the Bible: Song of Songs, Proverbs, and Ecclesiastes. Legends from the Talmud and Midrash, relating Solomon's knowledge of the language of animals and his power over demons, are included in:

Bialik, H. N., and Rawnitsky, Y. H., editors.
The Book of Legends. New York: Schocken, 1992.

Ginzberg, Louis. *The Legends of the Jews,* Volumes 4 and 6.
Philadelphia: Jewish Publication Society of America, 1948.

ELIE WIESEL is the author of more than forty books of fiction and nonfiction, including *Night*; *Dawn*; *A Beggar in Jerusalem*; *Souls on Fire*; and *Sages and Dreamers*. His most recent work is *Memoirs: All Rivers Run to the Sea*. He is Andrew Mellon Professor in the Humanities at Boston University. In 1986 Elie Wiesel received the Nobel Peace Prize.

MARK PODWAL is the author and illustrator of numerous books, which include *A Jewish Bestiary*; *The Book of Tens*; and *The Menorah Story*. He has collaborated with Elie Wiesel on various projects, including *A Passover Haggadah*; an illustrated limited edition of Professor Wiesel's collected works; and the video *A Passover Seder*, which was broadcast on public television.